LOVE
GOD'S GREATEST
GIFT

WRITTEN BY ~ STEVEN LAKE

LOVE: God's Greatest Gift
Copyright © 2016 by: Steven Lake
Written by: Steven Lake

Author Photo by: Steven Lake
Book Cover Design by: Donald Semora   www.donsemora.com

ISBN Number: 978-1-940155-39-5

10 9 8 7 6 5 4 3 2 1

Published by: Castle Top Publishing

Printed and Published in the United States of America

ACKNOWLEDGEMENTS

I would like to thank Pastor Richard Wilson and Susan VanLandt for their help in proofreading and editing the manuscript for this book. Their help, along with God's leading, has made this book possible.

INTRODUCTION

Love is something we cherish, seek out, remember fondly, long for, and enjoy. Love brings us joy, peace, happiness, and so much more. It's been explored in detail through the centuries by the likes of philosophers, theologians, scientists, poets, playwrights, politicians, lovers, and many others. It's among the most sought after things in this world. Yet so few really understand it. So that then begs a very important question. What truly constitutes love? To know the answer to this we must first explore what love is.

WHAT IS LOVE?

Love is many things to many people. To some it's sensual, to others it's an emotion, or an action, or even something entirely unique and indescribable in words. But I would like to conclude that love is far beyond just those simple definitions which neatly tuck it into a well-tailored box. In the simplest terms, and in its most elemental form, love is not a belief, or an attraction, or even a thought. Love is both an emotion and an action. But how can that be? Isn't it one or the other? No, this is not an either/or proposition. As with any emotion, in order to be known it must be expressed, otherwise it is of no substance or consequence. In other words, it must be both felt and expressed in physical action in order to be truly known. To love and yet not express it is to not love at all. Some might say this strictly makes love an action. Again, that's not true. To act, one must first be led to act. Therefore the action and the emotion are inseparable from one another.

That's why people in love do the things they do, both good and bad. It's also why God sent His only Son to die for us, which is arguably the single greatest expression of love ever! If He didn't love us, He would've simply tossed us in Hell and been done with the whole messy affair before it ever got started. In fact, if He hadn't loved us from the very beginning, even before we were made, He wouldn't have bothered to make us in the first place. This is especially important given all that He knew about us and what we'd do before we were ever made, right down to the tiniest of details. This is because, by nature God is love, and the ultimate expression of it. Sure, it's true that God is also just and holy, but if He were not, this world would not be worth living in, nor would eternity.

But at the same time I would like to submit to you that the justice which He holds to so dearly is also an extension of His love. If your child is doing something that may prove harmful to them, do you not chastise or punish them in hopes of ridding their mind and life of that destructive habit or belief? If you're a good parent, you will. Therefore, if God loves us (which He does), wouldn't it also be reasonable to assume that He would use chastisement or punishment to correct our ways when we're wrong to stop or prevent us from doing that which can or might harm us now or in the future? God doesn't wish for anyone to go to Hell. He gets absolutely no satisfaction in doing it. Even so He must balance His love for you with His holiness. But that still leaves us asking the question, what is love? What truly constitutes love? Perhaps Christ's own words said can shed some light on this.

John 14:15 (NIV) - *"If you love me, keep my commands."*

If you love Me, keep My commandments. This is such a simple verse, and yet speaks volumes to what I've already said above. "If you love Me" speaks of love as an emotion first, as I said before, and "Keep My commandments" in turn tells us how best to express this love. Therefore love by itself is nothing. However, love expressed is powerful and important, and what must occur for love to be real and not just a fleeting thought. Therefore if Christ is implying that if we do in fact love Him that we must also back that up with action, namely obedience, how much do we truly love the Lord, and in what ways can we, or do we express that love? In the next series of sections I plan to explore this topic and show you some of the ways we can express our love for God and others. Also through these chapters I will further reveal the greater nature, trademarks and traits of true, heartfelt, honest love.

POINTS FOR THOUGHT:

1. How do I view love? What is love to me?
2. How do I demonstrate love to others in my own life?
3. Do I truly love God? If so, how do I express that in my life?
4. Is my love truly genuine, or is it selfishly motivated?
5. How much does God love me? List each of the ways God has shown His love to you.

THE LOVE CHAPTERS

There are two key places in the bible (even though there are many hundreds of other verses on this topic) where the idea of love is directly defined. The first is known as "The Love Chapter", written by Paul the apostle, which outlines in detail some of the physical, actionable attributes of Love. The other one is called "The Great Commandment", which details how we are to love God and others. These two act as guideposts to help us understand what kind of love God expects us to show towards Him and others. So let's look at each of these and see what they say.

Matthew 22:37-40 (KJV) - *"Jesus said unto him, Thou shalt love the Lord thy God with **all** thy heart, and with **all** thy soul, and with **all** thy mind. This is the first and great commandment. And the second is like unto it, Thou shalt love thy neighbor as thyself. On these two commandments hang all the law and the prophets."* (emphasis mine)

This verse alone captures the entire essence of love. When you love, you are to do it with everything you have, and everything you are, towards God first and others second, leaving yourself last on the list. This can also be considered humility which, in its truest form, is another expression of love as you are putting others before yourself. That doesn't mean you have to become a doormat for someone. But it also doesn't mean you should be standoffish or anti-social either. Being humble and loving is a balancing act between your love for God and your love for others. In God's case, being perfect, He flawlessly understands both sides of that and in turn flawlessly executes it.

We, who are frail, failed, sinful, finite beings can only know and understand love in part. Even so, if you can love God, who you haven't seen, it then makes loving your neighbor, who you can see, all that much easier. This now brings us into the next set of love verses which detail in part some of the necessary actions or proofs to determine if one is properly loving God and others.

1 Corinthians 13:4-8a (NIV) - *"Love is patient, love is kind. It does not envy, it does not boast, it is not proud. It does not dishonor others, it is not self-seeking, it is not easily angered, it keeps no record of wrongs. Love does not delight in evil but rejoices with the truth. It always protects, always trusts, always hopes, always perseveres. Love never fails."*

That's a pretty high standard for loving, isn't

it? But it's *God's standard*, and as such we should aspire to live up to it. So what does it take to live a life of love? How do we go about living these two verses in our lives? Let's take a second and explore these verses point by point and expound a bit on what they can tell us about love, and in the process we should learn the answer to that.

POINTS FOR THOUGHT:

1. Memorize **Matthew 22:37-40** and also **1 Corinthians 13:4-8** and recite them to yourself daily.
2. Find ways to apply these two verses to your life daily.
3. Follow and exercise daily the points for demonstrating love laid out in these two verses.

LOVE IS PATIENT, IT IS NOT EASILY ANGERED

Colossians 3:12 (NIV) - *Therefore, as God's chosen people, holy and dearly loved, clothe yourselves with compassion, kindness, humility, gentleness and patience.*

Patience, single handedly, is one of the hardest of all the skills in life to master, and one of the most important as well. Impatience is, regrettably enough, a major portion of our lives. Yet it shouldn't be. If we truly love God and others, we should be patient in all things. Yet seemingly every day we find ourselves being impatient about all kinds of little things in our lives even if we don't think we're doing it. We're impatient about getting to work, even if we hate our job. We're impatient about seeing the doctor, even if we know it'll be bad news. We're impatient about seeing our children grow up, even though we only have a few precious years with them which go by far too quickly. We're impatient waiting in line for food. We're impatient waiting for the game to come on. We're even impatient while waiting for a simple, twenty second long traffic light to change. It seems like impatience is everywhere in our lives.

Even our patience is impatience because, while we're waiting patiently for something to happen, in the back of our minds we're wishing things would hurry up and happen already. In today's world of instant gratification we've lost the art and skill of patience. But in reality it's not so much that we've lost our patience as it is that we've lost our love. Allow me to explain. At the root of all impatience is the seemingly innocent act of frustration, which is a subset of the emotion of anger which can, if expressed improperly, be sinful and unrighteous. There is such a thing as righteous frustration and anger, as even Jesus said so. But more often than not ours is the other kind, the one that causes us to sin. This is because when we become impatient we become frustrated, and then angry, and then we sin, while at the same time becoming unloving to the person or thing of which we are being impatient.

There is also a factor of pride and arrogance measured into this impatience as well. It can be expressed in the concept of, "I'm better than this" or even the ever so grievous, "Do you know who I am!?" I'm sure many of you don't believe that you actually think or feel that way. But in reality you do, and probably far more often than you realize. For example, when going to eat at a restaurant, how often have you, at some point during your visit, asked the question, "Where's my food!?" Most of us do this, and rightly so as we're hungry. However, when it transforms from the simple inquiry of "where is my food?" to the equally worded, yet clearly impatient demand for information as though you're someone special, then it becomes impatience.

This is also where pride enters in, as the latter, if more correctly translated, isn't actually the question of "where is my food", but rather the much darker, and far more prideful question of, "Do you know who I am!? I am your paying customer and I want my food right now and if you don't give it to me this very instant I will walk out that door and leave you holding the bill!!" Now read that again, but do it with a snooty, snobbish voice. Now, after you've done that, if you take a really deep look into this, that's the exact question you're asking, with more or less the same attitude, even though it's not being expressed in those exact words. In short you're putting far more value on yourself than is rightfully due, and from that breeds impatience, pride and ultimately sin. Thus to be impatient is to be not only unloving, but also potentially prideful and arrogant because you are loving yourself more than the other person, and most especially God as your unloving actions to others are, in its most primal form, an act of unloving, prideful arrogance towards Him.

But before we go further, lets look at this from another angle. Let's say you've just brought home a brand new puppy who isn't potty trained yet, and at the same time loves to chew on sneakers. Now, fast forward two days, and in that short amount of time this sweet little puppy has already succeeded in peeing on the couch, not once, but five times in a row, all while simultaneously destroying two of your best pairs of shoes, turning them into the equivalent of a shredded tennis ball. What do you do with the puppy at that point? Would you gently correct them and try to teach them that your couch is not a toilet and your shoes a chew toy? Unless you're some bridge troll who hates everyone, you almost certainly would be patient with them. Is it because they're just a puppy, or is it because you love them? Well, ask yourself this question.

If your adult dog did the same thing, would you immediately throw them to the curb, or would you instead scold them gently in hopes of seeing them change for the better? Unless this was a repeated, defiant, blatant act by the dog, I'd suspect the latter. As such, that my friends, is love. How so? Because you're expressing patience towards them. But you might say, "No I'm not! I just know that they don't know any better because they're a puppy!" or "Well, he just had an accident" or some other excuse. Perhaps, but think deeper. Why did you bring that puppy home? It sure wasn't because you wanted someone to tear up your shoes or ruin your fifteen hundred dollar sofa.

You brought them home because you fell in love with them, and as such you will naturally express patience with them. Therefore, the more you love, the more patient you are. Case in point. I've seen men who love their wives so much that their wife can abuse them in ways that seem completely insane, and yet the husbands will display a grace and patience with them that defies logic. Why? Because, despite all the wife is doing, their love for her is so great that they'd gladly take a bullet for her, despite how she's treating them. That, my friends, is love, expressed magnificently through the act of patience. So to summarize, love breeds patience. Anger, pride and hatred on the other hand breed impatience. With that in mind, let's look at this verse again.

Matthew 22:37-40 (KJV) - *"Jesus said unto him, Thou shalt love the Lord thy God with all thy heart, and with all thy soul, and with all thy mind. This is the first and great commandment. And the second is like unto it, Thou shalt love thy neighbor as thyself. On these two commandments hang all the law and the prophets."*

Is this starting to make sense now? If you

love, you will be patient. If you do not love, you will not be patient. That is why love is patient. It is just a natural outgrowth of what love truly is. And it goes back to what I stated above about how the emotion of love, when fully expressed, becomes action. Thus what we do is a direct expression of what is in our hearts. If we truly love God, and we truly love others, patience becomes natural and we become gracious to others in ways that goes beyond our sinful, prideful human nature.

POINTS FOR THOUGHT:

1. At what points in my life am I impatient? (be completely honest with this.)
2. If I find that I'm impatient in anything, why am I impatient? What reasons are there that make me that way?
3. What steps can I take to reduce or eliminate impatience in my life?
4. Are the problems that are causing my impatience a lack of love towards the other person? Perhaps selfishness, pride, jealousness or a deep hatred I won't admit?
5. Whenever you find yourself being impatient with God, stop for a moment and praise Him for all He's done for you, especially His patience with you. Then ask forgiveness for your impatience.

Finally, ask Him to help you love Him more.

6. Remember that anytime God makes you wait, it's because He has something better for you.

7. Whenever you find yourself being impatient with others, ask yourself why you're impatient with them? Or why is it that you can't love them fully? Is it truly them, or is it instead your own pride and selfishness?

LOVE IS KIND

Ephesians 4:32 (KJV) - *"And be ye kind one to another, tenderhearted, forgiving one another, even as God for Christ's sake hath forgiven you."*

Kindness is another of the many elements of love, and one of the many ways it can be expressed to others, and especially to God. Being kind, and in some cases showing mercy, to others is a way of demonstrating that you love God. Because, as He was kind and merciful to you, in turn you should be kindly and mercifully to others. A good example of this comes from a parable by Jesus about a good Samaritan who, although despised by many in Christ's day, showed others what the true meaning of love was through one simple act of mercy.

Luke 10:30-35 (KJV) - *"And Jesus answering said, A certain man went down from Jerusalem to Jericho, and fell among thieves, which stripped him of his raiment, and wounded him, and departed, leaving him half dead. And by chance there came down a certain priest that way: and when he saw him, he passed by on the other side. And likewise a Levite, when he was at the place, came and looked on him, and passed by on the other side. But a* *certain Samaritan, as he journeyed, came where he was: and when he saw him, he had compassion on him, And went to him, and bound up his wounds, pouring in oil and wine, and set him on his own beast, and brought him to an inn, and took care of him. And on the morrow when he departed, he took out two pence, and gave them to the host, and said unto him, Take care of him; and whatsoever thou spendest more, when I come again, I will repay thee."*

So, in the same way that the Samaritan, and ultimately Jesus, showed mercy to others, it is expected of us to be kind and merciful to others. Not a kindness that feeds selfish, sinful needs, greeds, or desires, but rather a kindness that says, "Even if you are unlovable, I will demonstrate my love by being kind and merciful to you." Whoever expresses true kindness shows without question that the love of Christ is in their heart! And also through kindness we put God first and Others second, which is the antithesis of pride, which puts itself first, and displays neither mercy, nor kindness.

Sure, there are people who are not Christians, and not saved by Christ, who are kind people. But that kindness is always driven by an internal selfishness that is only nice to others so long as it's in their best interests to do so. But true kindness, the type that flows out of the heart of a redeemed person, is never selfish. It seeks to do God's will by demonstrating Christ's love to others, and showing through example that He loves them, and you, unconditionally. In doing so they also show obedience to Christ's command to love God with all their heart, and their neighbor as themselves.

POINTS FOR THOUGHT:

1. How do I define kindness and mercy?
2. How can I show kindness and mercy to others?
3. Is my kindness and/or mercy driven by selfishness or true love?
4. How can I show Christ's love towards others through my kindness?

IT DOES NOT ENVY

In the book of Exodus God gives Moses, the leader of the nation of Israel at that time, His ten commandments for each of them to live by. Among those ten commandments is listed one that warns us against committing one of the most destructive sins we can commit.

Exodus 20:17 (KJV) - *"You shall not covet your neighbor's house. You shall not covet your neighbor's wife, or his male or female servant, his ox or donkey, or anything that belongs to your neighbor."*

Envy is the desiring of someone else's things. The Old English word for this is "Covet". It can also be known as jealousy. Either way, envy itself is clearly viewed as a sin by God, and anyone who truly loves God and others will not be envious. Why? Because you will love the person, and not the things that they have. But let's explore that a little further, as wanting what someone else has can be both sinful, and not sinful. Allow me to explain. Envy, by proper definition, is wanting *the specific thing* that someone else has.

Desire on the other hand is merely wanting something *like* what the other person has. There's a big difference between the two. Case in point. Let's say that your neighbor just bought a new car, and it happens to be the exact make, mode, and color that you wanted. Saying, "I want one just like his," isn't envy. That's desire, which according to the bible is completely allowable. In fact, we're told to desire the things of God, but not to envy.

Psalm 37:4 (KJV) - *"Delight thyself also in the Lord: and he shall give thee the desires of thine heart."*

Matthew 5:6 (KJV) - *"Blessed are they which do hunger and thirst after righteousness: for they shall be filled."*

Psalm 119:20 (KJV) - *"My soul breaketh for the longing that it hath unto thy judgments at all times."*

Hebrews 10:5 (KJV) - *"Wherefore when he cometh into the world, he saith, Sacrifice and offering thou wouldest not, but a body hast thou prepared me."*

Psalm 119:40 (KJV) - *"Behold, I have longed after thy precepts: quicken me in thy righteousness."*

To desire is not sinful. So saying, for example, "I want a job *like* his," isn't envy. However, "I want *his* job," can be. It depends on what you mean. Do you want his *specific* job, or do you want one similar or identical to his? The fore is envy, the latter is desire. See what I'm getting at? There's a thin line between the two. One is sin, and one is merely an interest in being like someone you look up to, or having something similar or parallel to what they have. So feel free to desire things, but do not envy what God has given to others. God has a specific reason why He allowed them to have the things they do, and since you don't know what that exact reason is, it is best to trust that it's in your best interests that God kept it from you.

So don't envy what someone else has. There's a very good reason why you don't have it, and one you should be thankful for, even if you don't know or understand what that is. Now here is something that might blow your mind, but at the same time may not given what I stated above. Did you know that you can envy and be jealous and not sin? I bet that just blew your mind. So how can two things, which without reservation are seen as sinful, ultimately have a righteous, sinless use?

Exodus 20:3 (NIV) - "*You shall have no other gods before me.*"

Did you know that God is jealous? He even admits as much. Yet God is perfect, right? So how can He be jealous and yet sin not? Doesn't the bible say you can be angry and sin not?

Ephesians 4:26a (KJV) - *"Be ye angry, and sin not."*

So how is it possible, in the same way as anger, to be jealous and sin not? I think the biggest confusion here comes from a failure of the English language. Quite often we use the same word and apply numerous meanings to it that can only be discovered by viewing the full context of what is being said. Take the word "bear" for example. It's both a noun and a verb, and carries with it several uniquely different meanings as a result. For example, you can "bear" one's burdens, or you can meet a "bear" in the woods. Depending on the context the meanings are entirely different. Let's look at one example of this in the bible by going back and digging into the original text for some clues.

Exodus 20:5 (KJV) - *"Thou shalt not bow down thyself to them, nor serve them: for I the Lord thy God am a jealous God, visiting the iniquity of the fathers upon the children unto the third and fourth generation of them that hate me;"*

If you look closely at this verse in the original texts, you'll discover that the word for jealousy is the Hebrew word *"qanna"* which comes from the root word *"qinah"* which carries with it the idea of zeal. However, in Exodus 20:17 the word for covet (aka jealousy or envy) is "*epithumeó*" which means to lust after. So while the English language fails us in understanding the differences, the Hebrew comes to the rescue for us. So when God says don't be jealous of your neighbors stuff, but then turns around and says I am a jealous God, He's not being contradictory or schizophrenic. If you read it in the original text He's being very clear on His meaning. So you can be jealous (zealous) for the things of God and not sin, yet be jealous (lustful) for the things of your neighbor and end up sinning.

So to clarify this a bit further, using far more appropriate English words, you can be zealous for something, such as the things of God, and sin not. But you can't be lustful for the things of others and not sin. Lust in itself is a sin as it is impossible to lust and to love. They're completely incompatible as lust seeks to feed the flesh and hurt others while love seeks to bless others while denying the flesh. Plus, when you get right down to it, envy and jealousy are simply the physical manifestations of the idolatry that is in one's heart.

Romans 1:25 (KJV) - *"Who changed the truth of God into a lie, and worshipped and served the creature more than the Creator, who is blessed for ever. Amen."*

Right there is the rub when it comes to jealousy and envy. By being envious or jealous of someone else or what they have makes that thing you're envious of an idol in your life, and where your heart is, there is your treasure also.

Matthew 6:21 (KJV) - *"For where your treasure is, there will your heart be also."*

Matthew 6:24 (KJV) - *"No man can serve two masters: for either he will hate the one, and love the other; or else he will hold to the one, and despise the other. Ye cannot serve God and mammon."*

Loving *things*, which is essentially what envy and jealousy are, is one of the fastest ways to lose whatever love you have for others.

Exodus 20:3 (NIV) - *"You shall have no other **gods** before me."*

You shall have no other *gods* before Me. Think about that. Could it be that the real reason you're jealous or envious of what someone else has is because you've made that item an idol in your life? And if so, then you have not only lost your love for others, but also your love for God. This is because love and envy can't live in the same place. So what is the easiest way to regain your love for God and others? By putting yourself into last place where you belong, something that is otherwise known as the

JOY principle. IE, Jesus First, Others Second, Yourself Last. With this you will not only have love and real joy, but will also purge envy and jealousy from your life.

And lastly, one final thing to consider. Nothing in this world belongs to anyone except God. Thus, if you are only the steward of what God has given you, why be jealous of the things He has given to someone else to be the steward of. Remember, to whom much is given, much will be required. So the more they are given, the more they will be responsible for before God, having to give account for what they did with those blessings. So if God gives you less than your neighbor, be thankful. It's less you have to be responsible for in the end.

POINTS FOR THOUGHT:

1. Who in my life do I most envy? Why do I envy them?
2. What do they have that makes me jealous of them, or desiring of what they have?
3. Why do I want that item so badly?
4. Do I love that item more than God? Has it become an idol to me?
5. If God has not given me stewardship of that item or thing I desire most, why?
6. Is that item that I envy harmful to me, either physically or spiritually?
7. Is the reason God is withholding something from me because I'm not ready now to be a proper steward of the thing I desire most?

IT DOES NOT BOAST, IT IS NOT PROUD

Pride is the sin that caused Satan to fall. It's the sin that caused Adam and Eve to fall. It is the chief and highest of all sins, and it's what leads us to sin every single hour of every single day. It's the sin that destroys love in our hearts, because it causes us to take our eyes off of God and others, and wrongly put it onto ourselves. It is the most vile of all sins because it destroys everything it touches. It's selfishness personified. It's the sin that puts us first in our minds above all other things, including God, and it's the sin that comes easiest to us, and is the one we must fight the hardest to overcome.

Romans 12:10 (NIV) - *Be devoted to one another in love. Honor one another above yourselves.*

Boastfulness, which is an extension of pride, is the verbalization of its parent emotion. Just like love is only known by the actions one expresses, pride is known in the same way, and boastfulness is the verbal expression of pride. So where pride is the emotion, boastfulness is the action. It's like the antithesis of love, where love is patient, pride is impatient, as well as boastful, self serving, and many other things. However, one must also understand that, like with anger, not all boasting is wrong. There is a kind that is right in the eyes of God. How so? Well, boastfulness itself is merely an act that glorifies or lifts up something or someone else. So by itself it's not sinful. What is being boasted about, how that boasting is being done, and why one is doing it however can be. So if one is boasting (ie, glorifying) oneself, it's sin. If you're boasting about God or others, then it's not a sin, and therefore it's perfectly alright for you to do.

1 Corinthians 1:31 (KJV) - *"That, according as it is written, He that glorieth, let him glory in the Lord."*

So therefore boasting, if done wrongly and/or selfishly, is sinful, and is also a signpost that points to the existence of pride in one's heart. But if done right it's one of the greater ways in which to praise God. It will also help you cast off your own sinful pride and humble yourself, and in doing so God will lift you up. Remember, if you lift yourself up, you *will* be brought low as nothing can keep you there. But if you humble yourself, God *will* lift you up, and when He does, nothing can bring you down.

1 Peter 5:6 (KJV) - *"Humble yourselves, therefore, under*

God's mighty hand, that he may lift you up in due time."

Matthew 23:11 (KJV) - *"But he that is greatest among you shall be your servant."*

Luke 14:8-11 (KJV) - *"When someone invites you to a wedding feast, do not take the place of honor, for a person more distinguished than you may have been invited. If so, the host who invited both of you will come and say to you, 'Give this person your seat.' Then, humiliated, you will have to take the least important place. But when you are invited, take the lowest place, so that when your host comes, he will say to you, 'Friend, move up to a better place.' Then you will be honored in the presence of all the other guests. For all those who exalt themselves will be humbled, and those who humble themselves will be exalted."*

It is not for us to raise ourselves up. God alone reserves that right. We therefore must live in humbleness, always taking the lowest place, and to present ourselves least among everyone. If we humble ourselves, God will reward us. But why? Because in God's eyes those who are least are those who love the most and are also the greatest of all servants, and vice versa. It's the principle of love. If you truly love someone, you'll put them first in your life. However, don't fake or pretend to be humble just for the sake of gaining a reward as God knows your heart and the true intents of your actions.

If you pretend to be humble, God will treat that as pride and judge you accordingly. And never think of yourself as humble, because the moment you do, you lose your humility. But if you truly love God and others, you will naturally be humble, as humility is an outgrowth of love. So in a sense your humility is a barometer of your heart. The more you love God and others, the more humble you will become. So if you're looking for someone who truly loves God, and is a proper Christ follower, look for those with true humility, and not a false banner that proclaims them to be.

If they say, "Look at me!" or "Look who I am!" or "Look what I've done!", then they are not humble. Remember, love does not boast, nor is it proud. To truly love, there can be no pride in your heart, nor can there be any boastfulness in your life, save for the boasting we do in the Lord. So if we put God and others first in our lives, then God will take the love in our hearts and expand it, leaving no place anywhere in our lives for pride to settle down and take root.

POINTS FOR THOUGHT:

1. Am I prideful or boastful of myself?
2. Do I automatically put God and others before myself, or do I do it because I have to? IE, do I force myself to do it?
3. Who gets the most glory in my life? Is it myself, or is it God?
4. Do most of my answers begin with "I" or "Me" or "My", or do they begin with "God" and "His"?
5. Is my thoughts focused on what *I* can do for *myself*, or it it on what can I do to server God and others?
6. Is there any area of my life in which pride is apparent? Even the tiniest bit of leaven (ie, pride) can leaven (ie, ruin) the entire loaf (ie, your life).
7. Is my love for God greater than my love for myself?

IT DOES NOT DISHONOR OTHERS

What does it mean to dishonor others as the bible says? Well, in the King James Version the word "Dishonor" is replaced by the word "Unseemly." This in its simplest definition means to behave rudely, or act inappropriately, in ways that bring dishonor, embarrassment or shame to someone else. If you dishonor someone else you hurt them. This firmly goes against the principle that "you do not hurt those whom you love". God loves us, and if we dishonor Him by acting defiant, sinful, belligerent, or just outright unloving and wrong, we dishonor Him.

We can easily do the same to others, doing things that bring shame to them. There are two ways we can do this. We can either do it intentionally in a spiteful way, with the intention of harming them (or Him) or we can do it accidentally with our actions, not knowing that what we've said or done is wrong. But when is what we do really dishonor, and when is it not? Well, the first question to ask is, "Does it harm the other person, or does it bless them?" Things that would harm someone else might be as simple as telling what many call "a little white lie", or going much further into horrible sins such as racial or social slurs, lying, cheating, stealing, or worse.

However, telling the truth is not hurtful. In fact, telling the truth, the honest truth, is beneficial. I'm not saying that telling them what *you* think is the truth isn't harmful. I'm talking about honest facts, things that are set in stone and can't be altered by either your opinion or what you believe to be true. For example, if you called someone fat and ugly, that's just your opinion of them. The facts and realities of that individual might be entirely different, as there are truths that are unquestionable, unchangeable, and unmovable, such as what Jesus did for us on Calvary. But our opinions are merely the expression of how we view the world, and are often colored with half truths and outright lies that we have come to believe either through our own naivety, or our personal prejudices. So when we share or treat them as "gospel truth" we in turn bring dishonor to others.

So always remember, be loving and compassionate to others, stick to the truth, the real truth, and don't be unseemly or hurtful to others. Also, don't be surprised when you offend some people, even though that was never your intention. Some people will be hurt and offended no matter what you do. You can't get around that. To some simply sharing the Gospel is hurtful to some, not because it brings any form of dishonor to others, but rather because the truth of it shines a powerful light onto the sins in their life they would rather not be seen. So if you are sharing truth in love, you will not dishonor others, even if they feel hurt for you doing so. If they become offended, it's because they offended themselves, and not you. So seek to love everyone, always share the gospel, and never act in a way that is selfish or dishonoring to others. For if you love others, and you especially love God, you will never willingly or intentionally hurt or dishonor someone.

POINTS FOR THOUGHT:

1. How do I act towards others? Is it right and appropriate, or is it sinful?
2. Are any of my actions naturally and sinfully hurtful to others?
3. Am I calling out their sin in an effort to hurt them, or is it to warn them of the dangers that come from exercising that sin?
4. Do I love them enough to share Christ with them in the hope of rescuing them from Hell, or am I too afraid or selfish to step out and do what God has commanded?

IT IS NOT SELF-SEEKING

To be self-seeking is, by definition, to be selfish. IE, you put yourself and your needs above that of others. It's the opposite of the JOY principle that I've spoken of many times before which puts Jesus First, Others Second, and Ourselves Last. It takes JOY and turns it into YOJ, which is neither a word, nor the right way to do things. If you put yourself before either Jesus or others or both, it ceases to be JOY and just becomes a convoluted mess. That's why keeping the proper order and perspective is always important. As a means of application to point out the importance of this, allow me to use a nautical example. My story begins with a guy named Bob who's taking a trip on a cruise ship. One day by accident it strikes a large rock and begins sinking. Immediately the crew orders everyone to climb into a life boat for their safety. Bob does so obediently, but before anyone else can get in, including any crew members, he pulls the release cord and down into the water goes the boat.

Why did he do this? Because he was selfish and didn't care who got left behind. He just wanted to get off the boat and to safety as soon as possible, no matter the cost. Well, he did succeed at this goal of fleeing to safety and can now comfortably sit back and watch the ship sink from a distance in the safety of the cabin of his life boat. However, there's just one problem. Because of what he did, he will now die a slow, painful death. Why? Because, without a crew member to activate and pilot the life boat, or activate any of its safety systems, such as the boat motor, the emergency beacon or anything, his life boat is useless to him. This is because, to start the boat requires a crew member with a special key. However, they went down with the ship, and took the key with them. Now Bob has found himself lost at sea with a useless boat that will almost invariably sink before he is rescued, and all because he was selfish and self-seeking, only thinking of himself, seeking to put himself before others in all cases. And in the end, one selfish, self-seeking act has not only doomed him, but also everyone else that could have been saved had he not done what he did.

Now some might argue the finer points of this by saying, "That's not how life boats work!" Maybe they do, and maybe they don't. The point is, one person crawled in, and that one person lowered the boat without anyone else in it, meaning that instead of forty people being carried to safety, thirty nine died and one lived. Or at least he will for a little while as in this scenario he too would die, just not as swiftly. Or, if that's not impactful enough, let's take this a little closer to home. Let's say you're driving down the road and see an accident in front of you. The car perhaps hit a patch of black ice, spun out and hit a tree. It's on fire and the driver is trapped. But you just drive by because you don't want to be bothered, or you're late for work or a meeting and you care more about your job than you do about the stranger who is about to die a fiery death.

Love is not that way. Love is others-seeking, and never self-seeking. We always put others before ourselves if we truly love them. But who are these "others" I'm speaking of. Jesus called them our "neighbors". That of course then begs the ages old question, "Who is my neighbor?" Of course, now that we've asked that question I will allow Jesus Himself to answer that once again using the story of the Good Samaritan as our example.

Luke 10:30-35 (KJV) - *"And Jesus answering said, A certain man went down from Jerusalem to Jericho, and fell among thieves, which stripped him of his raiment, and wounded him, and departed, leaving him half dead. And by chance there came down a certain priest that way: and when he saw him, he passed by on the other side. And likewise a Levite, when he was at the place, came and looked on him, and passed by on the other side. But a certain Samaritan, as he journeyed, came where he was: and when he saw him, he had compassion on him, And* *went to him, and bound up his wounds, pouring in oil and wine, and set him on his own beast, and brought him to an inn, and took care of him. And on the morrow when he departed, he took out two pence, and gave them to the host, and said unto him, Take care of him; and whatsoever thou spendest more, when I come again, I will repay thee."*

So who was this person the Samaritan saved? Was he actually someone who lived next door, a true neighbor as we think of them? Hardly. Not only were they from different regions, they were even of different heritages. The Samaritans were what one could call a "half blood Jew". i.e., they were Jews of old who'd intermarried with women from the surrounding areas and nations. To a regular Jew they were the most despised and hated of all the races, and they in turn hated the Jews as well. There was probably more animosity between these two groups than there was between anyone else, including the Jews and Romans, or even the Greeks from which came Antiochus Epiphanes, the madman, the same insane leader of the Seleucid Greek empire that desecrated the Jewish temple resulting in the Maccabean revolt and the holiday of Hanukkah.

To get a better perspective on how badly these two groups hated each other, take a moment, close your eyes and picture the most hated, vile, disgusting, wretched thing you know of. Go ahead, close your eyes and bring that to the forefront of your mind. Do you feel the hatred, anger and disgust that brings to your heart? Now, magnify that ten fold and you'd begin to get an idea of how badly they hated each other. Jews traveling north would go out of their way to go *around* Samaria just so they didn't have to go through the "filthy, smelly" land of the Samaritans. Now you kinda see why this message was such a shock to those listening to it at that time. Yet in the parable that Jesus told, this same hated person, who by rights should have equally hated the wounded Jewish man he found along the road, instead took time out of is day to help the man, even going so far as to clean and bind up his wounds, and see to the care of all his injuries!

To use a more modern equivalent, that'd be like a Jew binding the wounds of a Nazi Waffen SS officer and seeing to his injuries despite the fact that the Nazi wants him dead. Or perhaps a black man tending to the wounds of the same Klansman who just tried to lynch him. To the normal human mind this is not logical. It goes against everything that we think is normal and proper. We think, "Hey, he tried to kill me, so he deserves to be left alone to die!" But that's not what love does. Love cares for the other person, even if they do not care for you. They may want you dead, and may succeed at it. But even so we are to follow the example of Christ to the letter, following His example to the letter, never being self seeking, but always being others-seeking.

And it doesn't need to be displayed via the more graphic demonstrations I've listed above. I only gave those as examples of what this principle would look like if taken to its most extreme potential. So being either self-serving or others-serving can be seen in things as simple as holding the door for someone else, paying for someone else's meal, feeding the homeless, deferring to a co-worker, or even an enemy, being nice to them, blessing them in numerous ways, and even going so far as to help them climb up the corporate ladder above you, promoted before and above you, even perhaps into the same place you wanted to go. And the same can be said with Jesus, since He is to be placed in our lives in the very highest place above all others.

So basically put, when we follow the JOY principle, which believe it or not is biblical (remember Matthew 22:37-40 and what it said?), we will not only show love to others by NOT being self-serving, but we will also be following the principle of JOY to the letter, which always leads back to Christ.

One way to understand this is to view it this way. When I serve Jesus I directly serve God. When I serve others, I serve Jesus by serving them. And I serve Jesus by keeping myself last of all, as it keeps me humble and reminds me that if I am to love properly I am neither to be first, for that place is strictly held by Jesus, nor second, as that place is held by others, and them alone.

To be self-serving is unloving because you put yourself higher up on the list than you rightly should be. That is not to say you're less of a person if you put yourself last, but rather that it helps you keep a right perspective, and helps maintain a proper degree of humility in all things.

POINTS FOR THOUGHT:

1. What things must I do in my life to always put Jesus first?
2. What things must I do in my life to always put others second?
3. In doing #2, how must I serve others such that in doing so I am also serving Christ?
4. Through all of this am I keeping a proper level of humility in all that I do?

IT KEEPS NO RECORD OF WRONGS

What does it mean to keep a record of wrongs? Well, it's more than just simple note taking, or records keeping. It is, in its simplest terms, unforgiveness. If we keep in our minds, or sometimes even on paper, a record of all the wrongs someone has done to us, then we ourselves have expressed a lack of forgiveness, and ultimately a hatred towards the other person. Because, where there is hate, love cannot exist. Christ expressed this fact very strongly many times in the gospels.

Matthew 18:21-35 (NIV) - *"Then Peter came to Jesus and asked, "Lord, how many times shall I forgive my brother or sister who sins against me? Up to seven times?" Jesus answered, "I tell you, not seven times, but seventy-seven times. Therefore, the kingdom of heaven is like a king who wanted to settle accounts with his servants. As he began the settlement, a man who owed him ten thousand bags of gold was brought to him. Since he was not able to pay, the master ordered that he and his wife and his children and all that he had be sold to repay the debt. At this the servant fell on his knees before him.*

'Be patient with me,' he begged, 'and I will pay back everything.' The servant's master took pity on him, canceled the debt and let him go. But when that servant went out, he found one of his fellow servants who owed him a hundred silver coins. He grabbed him and began to choke him. 'Pay back what you owe me!' he demanded.

His fellow servant fell to his knees and begged him, 'Be patient with me, and I will pay it back.' But he refused. Instead, he went off and had the man thrown into prison until he could pay the debt. When the other servants saw what had happened, they were outraged and went and told their master everything that had happened. Then the master called the servant in. 'You wicked servant,' he said, 'I canceled all that debt of yours because you begged me to. Shouldn't you have had mercy on your fellow servant just as I had on you?' In anger his master handed him over to the jailers to be tortured, until he should pay back all he owed. This is how my heavenly Father will treat each of you unless you forgive your brother or sister from your heart."

That's pretty strong words, isn't it? It almost sounds like Jesus is saying that, if we don't forgive others in the same way God has forgiven us we'll lose our salvation. I'm not saying that's the message being given here. But even if it's not, it should still give us all the more motivation to literally ensure that we do all we can to "keep no record of wrongs" in any way, shape or form. But in reality, why should we keep a record in the first place? Is not every single one of us a fallen creature, and all of us sinners of the blackest sort? Is not even our greatest righteousness as vile and disgusting as dung before God? As such, shouldn't holding a sin against someone else be among the highest degree of hypocrisy, as we are just as sinful and guilty of evil as the one against whom we've kept our record of wrong?

As long as we're living in this sin cursed world we are and will always remain sinful, flawed human beings until the day in which we either die, or are raptured away to Heaven where we will, for the first time ever, become truly sinless creatures living inside perfect, flawless bodies entirely devoid of the sin nature that pervades us now. Until then we are all sinful creatures. Even if we've been saved and transformed, our sin nature still lurks within us. So don't hold any record of wrongs against anyone else. Correct them if you must, but do it in love, lifting up and edifying them in a way that blesses them, and draw them closer to Christ. We should do the same with those who are lost. As has been said by many in times past, "Love them into the kingdom."

Think about that. People are naturally attracted to love. Why is that? Because they deal with so much hate and unforgiveness in the world that love becomes a welcome beacon of light that pierces through the pitch blackness surrounding them. It's like a moth to the flame, only this is a light of love and hope for them. Therefore, if we're unforgiving to others, how are we any different than the world? If someone wants to see unforgiveness all they need to do is look in the mirror or even to their own neighbors, coworkers, or family. But if we display forgiveness, we are set apart from the world as Christ was and is, desiring not to be like the lost, but to display brightly and clearly to all that we're different, because we've been truly redeemed and that God's love flows through us. So hold no grudges, don't be unforgiving, and never let the sun go down on your anger.

And if you do find yourself angry with someone, ask yourself why. What did they do that made you mad and unforgiving? If you look deep enough, and search for the true reasons that you are unforgiving, you'll almost always discover that it was your **_pride_** that was wounded, and not your heart. Thus why you're unforgiving. If you should discover that to be true, then be wise and cast your pride aside and let it die where it lays. Once you've done that forgive the person for what they've done.

If you find that you can't forgive them, do it anyways. If you still can't, then praise God, and worship Him and ask that He change your heart. Then begin to say kind, uplifting, encouraging words of praise about the person you hate. It may be hard, but do it. In doing so it will turn your heart in the right direction, and eventually forgiveness will be possible. In fact, if you feel so inclined, consider thanking them for what they've done, because in making you angry they've just helped you both discover and cast out pride from your heart, which in many ways is a blessing to you.

One last thing. Forgiveness is a two way street. Not only do you have to forgive others, you must *forgive yourself*. That is likely the hardest thing anyone has or will ever ask you to do. If you think I'm kidding, I'm not. Examine yourself in detail. How often do you get down on yourself for things you've done in the past, especially mistakes, errors, wrong choices, or worse? "I can't believe I did that!" or "I wish I hadn't done that." Some call this regret, yet deep down it's unforgiveness of self. All of us suffer from it. Sometimes I feel like I'm the king of regret. There's so many mistakes I've made in my life that I wish I hadn't, and I can't even tell you how desperately I want to see them go away. That's regret and it's destructive to your soul. I've struggled with this myself for years. Yet God is slowly helping me forgive myself for those evils, even though it's been a long, hard road. I can't say it's easy. In fact, it's probably easier to forgive others than it is oneself. But it's something you must do, no matter how long it takes, ro how hard it is.

Plus, unforgiveness gives room for the enemy, and we must never allow Satan to gain *any* ground whatsoever in our lives. That's why we must forgive ourselves for *all* of our past mistakes. If we're born again, Jesus has already forgiven them. So now we need to as well. I'm sure every one of us wish we could undo the mistakes of our past. But that's just it. We're failed, flawed human beings. We make mistakes. It's just who we are. They're going to happen no matter what we do or how hard we try. It's a side effect of our sinful, fallen nature. So we can't keep dwelling on them. Once they're forgiven we must in turn tear up the record we've been keeping and throw it away. Both the record of our own personal wrongs, as well as those done by others. Remember, love keeps no record of wrongs, either of your own or those of others.

Psalm 103:12 (KJV) - "*As far as the east is from the west, so far hath he removed our transgressions from us.*"

So let go of all wrongs, and keep no record of them, be they your own, or those done to you by another. Let them go and let God be king in your life. He forgave you of **_ALL_** your sins and saved you from Hell. Therefore we should cast all record of our past wrongs, and those of others, down the great majestic memory hole where they rightfully belong and never again pick up their dusty bones either now or at any point throughout eternity.

POINTS FOR THOUGHT:

1. Is there anyone in my life I have not forgiven?
2. Is there anyone in whom I hold a grudge?
3. Is there anyone (including myself) on whom I keep a list of wrongs?
4. Have you forgiven everyone who has sinned against you, including yourself?
5. Can you remember anything wrong that you or someone else has done? If you can, you haven't truly forgiven it, and you are also still keeping a list of wrongs. Resolve to forgive it, forget it, and be done with it, never to pick it up again.
6. Never look to the past and what you could've done. Always look to the future and what you *can* do right now for God and others.

LOVE DOES NOT DELIGHT IN EVIL BUT REJOICES WITH THE TRUTH

How many times have you seen someone cheer when something bad happens to someone else? Or how many times have you seen people get excited when the idea of committing a blatant sin is introduced to them? Those are just two of the many ways in which people delight in evil. But, if we are born again believers, that should not be us. We should always rejoice in holiness, goodness and the truth, and even rejoice in God's judgments, as they are always right and true. But never should we ever rejoice in evil. To rejoice in evil is to give it legitimacy. Say your neighbor, who happens to be the "grumpiest man alive", gets in a car wreck and totals his vehicle, the same one he spent every day fawning over, or even perhaps flaunting in your face.

If you cheer because his vehicle got wrecked, you're rejoicing in evil. Or let's say that the guy at work, the one everyone loves to hate, or the one who's always causing you headaches, gets fired. If you rejoice in this, you're delighting in evil, or rejoicing in it. That should not be so. The same goes with sin. If someone you know is living deep in sin, if you rejoice in that, or give your approval to it, then you're delighting in evil. Or how about getting drunk? If you do it, you're delighting in evil. What about pornography? That's a big one these days. One of the Ten Commandments given to Moses said, *"You shall not commit adultery."*

Matthew 5:27-28 (KJV) - *"Ye have heard that it was said by them of old time, Thou shalt not commit adultery: But I say unto you, That whosoever looketh on a woman to lust after her hath committed adultery with her already in his heart."*

I'm certain that most Christian men and women haven't committed physical adultery. Or at least they better not have. But how many have looked upon the opposite sex and lusted after them? If I were to ask for a show of hands, I'd expect to see everyone raising their hands. According to Jesus, if you do that you've committed adultery, and I'm sure all of us are guilty of that at some point in our lives, even if we don't want to admit it. Also, if we're truly honest with ourselves we should be forthright in admitting that it still plagues us today. I know I fight the sin of lust every single day of my life, even though it repulses me. But that's because we're human. We're drawn to the other sex like a magnet.

That's just who we are. Or at least who we were, as Christ has changed us and made us new inside. Even so Satan, the world and our old sin nature loves to club us over the head with a sledgehammer, constantly trying to suck us back down into sin.

But God has called us to resist that call of sin. So if Christ has renewed us, changed us, made us new creatures in Him, why oh why are we still tormented and tried by sin? Why does it have such an insanely powerful pull on us? Consider this possibility. Since love is an action, wouldn't it be reasonable that God would put us in a place where we'd have to willfully chose Him over the world? If we really love God, and especially Christ, shouldn't we do all within our power, and most especially through the power of Christ, to turn away from every sin, even the ones that have the most powerful pull on our lives, the ones we don't seem able to break free of? Love does not delight in evil, but rejoices with the truth. Chew on that one for a bit. That which you love is that which you will always turn to first, diligently seek out, immediately go to, and confide in every single time.

Therefore that which you love is that which you will go to first when certain needs or desires, which exist in our lives, cry out to be fed. But that then begs another question. What can we feed, and what should we starve? To begin with we first must understand that some needs in our lives are best controlled by feeding them, and others by starving them. How they're fed or starved though is what matters most. For example, when it comes to lust, the best way to deal with that is to starve it to death by engaging in intimacy with God through prayer and bible study every day, and then intimacy with your spouse if you're married, or outright abstinence and celibacy if you're not. We must never give any place in our lives for lust.

It must be starved to the point that it has no more power over us, no matter how hard we have to fight it, or for how long. And if we fail, we need to ask God for forgiveness, and then confess our sin to our spouse if we're married, or to a fellow brother (for men) or sister (for women) in Christ if we're single. This will give us a source of accountability, which we need if we're to defeat the evil of sins like lust, as well as many others.

Ephesians 4:31 (KJV) - *"Let all bitterness, and wrath, and anger, and clamour, and evil speaking, be put away from you, with all malice."*

To rejoice in evil is to hate God. Or if that love of evil is not directed towards a person, then it is directed towards God, as by rejoicing in evil, you have shown hatred to Him. Never rejoice in evil, but always rejoice in the truth, in goodness, in love, and all things that God loves.

2 Timothy 2:24 (ESV) - *"And the Lord's servant must not be quarrelsome but kind to everyone, able to teach, patiently enduring evil."*

1 Peter 3:8 (ESV) - *"Finally, all of you, have unity of mind, sympathy, brotherly love, a tender heart, and a humble mind."*

So the easiest way for us to never rejoice in evil and always rejoice in truth is to have our hearts and minds fixed and trained on Christ as well as all that is good and true.

Philippians 4:8 (ESV) - *"Finally, brothers, whatever is true, whatever is honorable, whatever is just, whatever is pure, whatever is lovely, whatever is commendable, if there is any excellence, if there is anything worthy of praise, think about these things."*

POINTS FOR THOUGHT:

1. In what areas of my life do I delight in evil?
2. How and when have I rejoiced in the truth?
3. Have I shown compassion to those who have suffered evil?
4. Have I rejoiced in and sought after truth in all things?
5. Does my mind dwell on things that are either evil or sinful, or does it seek out God and the things that He loves?

IT ALWAYS PROTECTS

Which of you, having a loved one, a child, a parent, a brother or sister, or someone else you love, wouldn't step up and do all to protect them, even going as far as giving your own life in their defense? I'm sure all of you would raise your hands were I to ask for a show of them. But what if protecting your loved ones instead involved something much, much simpler? What if it involved the food on your table or the cloths on their backs? If you love your children, don't you do all to provide for them? I would think that you do. Do you realize that, in its own way, your provision for them is a form of protection? This is because, by providing for them, you're shielding them from need, starvation, cold, heat, and all sort of other dangers; things they themselves might not be able to protect themselves from. That's what it means to protect: To shield another from harm, be that great or small, real or perceived. Christ did that for us on the cross.

He died to take away our sins to protect us from the wrath of God and from Hell (which we rightly deserve) and allow us to come legally and without fault into God's presence, and Heaven as well. But when does protection stop being loving? Or when can we still love the person, and yet rightly and necessarily withdraw our hand of protection from them? Well, there are two basic times when this can happen. The first is when punishment is required. God sometimes chastises us for our sins by withdrawing His hand of protection ever so slightly, allowing enough room for the Devil to come in and torment or harm us. Is God still protecting us? Absolutely! However, that slight lifting of His protection is not being done for our harm, but rather to teach us a lesson, or to train us in the right way to go, and to help us to make a necessary course correction so we're not sailing onto the jagged rocks of destruction.

This is because pain is one of the best motivators ever created. For those of you with children, what's been your greatest teachable moments? For most it's occurred when there's been some form of pain, be that emotional or physical, experienced by the child. Allowing someone to fall in order to learn a lesson is not a failure to protect. As we all have free will, we are also free to make our choices. But God, our Father, knows that not every choice we make is right. So He periodically steps back and allows us to go against His leading and His will, ultimately to the point in which we fail, with the intention of allowing us to learn a lesson from our mistakes. And by doing so He protects us from a potentially greater harm hard we continued down that same path.

Then, when we've learned that lesson, and have repented of our folly, God again wraps His loving, protective arms around us and holds us tight. But He'll only protect us as far as we'll let Him. Even so He'll still seek to protect us from harm because that which you love is that which you protect. He will also protect us from life's unexpected calamities, save only when suffering the effects of such an event is either to our benefit, God's glory, or both. For example, let's say that the company you work for goes out of business due to bad management, market shifts, they're downsizing, or you lose your job for other reasons not of your own making, such as mistakes or bad job performance.

Or perhaps something more pedestrian happens such as a deer or a moose steps out in front of your car, someone hits you, or you slide off the road and total your vehicle, or anything number of similar things like that. Did you walk away unhurt? Did your job loss force you to trust God more and draw closer to Him? Did it force you to make a change in your life you otherwise would not have made? If you did, praise God! And if you didn't, then God may have a positive use for that problem. As it says in the Bible, all things work for good to those who love God.

Romans 8:28 (KJV) - *"And we know that all things work together for good to them that love God, to them who are the called according to his purpose."*

Sometimes God allows bad things to happen to good people. But does that mean He's stopped loving you, and thus protecting you? Absolutely not! You didn't die, did you? But what if you had? Would it surprise you to know that in dying God protected you from something worse? He may even have used your death to reach someone else who wouldn't have come to a saving faith in Jesus Christ any other way. Therefore by dying God has graduated you into your eternal reward, and in turn protected someone else from Hell by providing the necessary circumstances to bring them to salvation. So while we don't know all the divine reasons why God let's some people die while saving others, if you are His child, death is always a blessing as what waits for you on the other side is far, far better than what exists here in this world for you were you to survive. However, if you're unsaved, your death is not for your protection, but is ultimately your judgment for rejecting Jesus Christ for the final time, having exhausted all of your available opportunities to be saved, having hardened your heart past the point of being saved.

Thus all that remains for you is punishment in Hell for all eternity. But if you're still alive, and unsaved, you still have time to get right with God. So don't delay, because death may be standing at the door ready to carry you into a Godless eternity, forever trapped in the fiery horrors of Hell. Now is the time of repentance. Now is the time of salvation. If you are reading this, and you have not given your heart to Christ, then know that God has indeed protected you to this very day because He loves you, otherwise you would not be here. But at some point, even though He still loves you, His protection must rightly lift, and should that day come for you because of your unrepentance and sinfullness, it will be a dark day for you beyond all comprehension.

So if God, who is love personified, protects us from harm and danger, how must we in turn act to protect those we love? To be unwilling to protect someone, be that physically, emotionally, spiritually or more, from harm and danger, be that of their own making, or from forces outside of themselves, is to hate them. To seek their protection, even if they don't want it, is to show that you care.

And remember, it doesn't have to be physical

protection that you give them. It can be a helping hand when help is needed, a word of advice or insight when wisdom is needed, food when they are hungry, friendship or kind words when they are sad or hurt, perhaps even a hug or a shoulder to cry on if you know them well enough, companionship when they are lonely, a warm place to stay when they are cold, direction when they are lost, or even simply water when they are thirsty. Always protect those you love, and see to their wellbeing and safety, and when you can't protect them, place them in God's hands, as He is the greatest protector of all. But here's an interesting final thought for you to chew on that may change the way you view God.

Did you know that every time you sin you hurt God? Yes, you hurt Him deeply. If you hurt Him through your sin, doesn't that mean you failed to protect the one you love? As crazy as it sounds, little finite you actually have the ability to protect the great God of the universe. But when you do it, you're not protecting someone weaker than you, because God is many multiple times greater than even this universe. Yet emotions are, in a way, the great equalizer. Again, I'm not saying I or anyone else is equal or superior in any way with God. He's always greater. Even so, anytime we sin it hurts Him greatly. When someone you love sins against you, doesn't it just rip you apart inside? God is no less hurt if we sin against Him.

So if we truly love God we will always strive for sinless perfection. Because if we love God, we will seek to protect Him from hurt by doing all we can not to sin against Him, because every time we sin we hurt Him. So striving to be sinless is to protect God from the heartache we cause Him when we sin. In a sense it's much the same thing as what a child would do for their parent. If they knew that sin or disobedience would cause their parents great anguish and hurt, would they not thus seek to be obedient to protect their parents from heartache and pain? That's what it's like when we seek to be faithful and sinless before God. Remember, love protects that which it loves.

POINTS FOR THOUGHT:

1. In what ways has God protected you from your follies?

2. How has God protected you from life itself? (ie, calamities not of your own making)

3. In what way do you protect others, be that friends, family, co-workers, or others?

4. Do you try to reach others with the Gospel to protect them from Hell by leading them to a saving knowledge of Christ?

5. Who do you love and wish to protect, but are unable to? Have you prayed for them? Have you put their safety in God's almighty hands?

LOVE ALWAYS TRUSTS

Trust is the center of all things in life. Trust is what makes it possible to go about our day. You might wonder how this is possible. Consider this idea. When you sit down in a chair, are you not trusting that it will hold up your weight? Or when a traffic light turns green and you proceed into the intersection, doesn't your actions indicate that you trust that it's safe to cross? Or when you pet your cat, do you trust it to be gentle with you and not either bite or scratch you? That's the basic tenants of trust. It's everywhere and in everything, and without it we wouldn't be able to go about our day. Yet trust in and of itself can operate separately from love. You can trust without loving, but you can't love without trusting. I know, strange concept, right?

But I don't think it's necessarily because trust must be present to be loving. Trust, in its simplest form, is a component of faith. Don't we quite regularly use the words faith and trust interchangeably? Or even together in the same sentence, using one word as a multiplier for the other? For example, when we walk people through the sinner's prayer, don't we often say, "Will you put your entire *faith* and *trust* in Jesus Christ?" Or how often have you said, "I have faith that you will do good," to someone? Now interchange that with the word trust. "I trust that you will do good." Did you notice that, despite the changing of words, the meaning conveyed is still the same? Now, read this pair of sentences and see if you feel the same thing from both.

"I trust you, but I don't love you."
"I love you, but I don't trust you."

Did they sound like they were conveying the same meaning, or a different one? Surprisingly enough, they both have the same meaning. Both are statements lacking love, despite the one statement claiming to love the other person. Why? Because, like I said above, you can trust someone and not love them, but you can't love them without trusting them. So if that's true, how does one reconcile situations where you do love someone else, however, due to things they've done, you've lost all trust in them? For example, a disobedient child or an unfaithful spouse? Well, let me ask you this. Do you still have faith that they can be changed or brought around to where they should be? If you said yes, then you still have faith in them, and thus trust.

Perhaps it's not the trust we typically think of, such as the trust we put in our chairs, but it's still trust. Remember, trust and faith are interchangeable. But both words also come with multiple meanings and applications. So probably the better way to say this would be that "Love Always Has Faith" rather than "Love Always Trusts". This idea is even backed up by the Koine Greek which uses the word "pisteuw" (pronounced pist-yoo'-o), which means "faith in, upon, or with respect to something." And, just as the words "trust" and "faith" share a common meaning, the Greek word "pisteuw" carries a duel meaning of both faith and trust.

So, stepping around the limitations of the English language when describing this concept, one only need replace the word "Trust" with "Faith" whenever one comes up against a seemingly difficult contradiction like this. Now here's another that you might have a little trouble dealing with.

"I love them, but I have no faith or trust in them."

Look at that statement and how it plays out. You "love" them, yet you are missing the one key element that truly makes it love. Namely, faith and/or trust in the individual. It's not possible to love someone without having at least some faith or trust in them. At this point all that remains is a hope that they will change in such a way that will permit you to love them again. And if you have hope, you may still have at least a little love for them. But that's another topic for another section. Ultimately though, we must have faith and trust in the other person to truly have authentic love for them.

Proverbs 3:5-6 (KJV) - *"Trust in the Lord with all thine heart; and lean not unto thine own understanding. In all thy ways acknowledge him, and he shall direct thy paths."*

In the same way we must trust and have faith in others in order to truly love them, we must also have faith and trust in the Lord our God if we are to truly love Him as He has called us to do. But if we are to lovingly trust the lord, what kind of love is it that we must express? Well, as is true of many words in the English language, the word *love* carries with it numerous meanings defined entirely by the context in which it's used rather than the word itself. Thankfully though, the Greek language has a great solution for this problem through the use of a variety of unique words that have very specific meanings. For example:

Agape
Unconditional Love

Eros
Erotic Love (like the kind expressed between a
husband and wife)

Philia
The kind of casual love we would most typically
refer to as "friendship".

Storge
The kind of love a parent expresses towards their
child or vice versa.

Ludus
We would understand this as a playful or "puppy"
type love.

Pragma
This is a love that's been around for a very long time.

So which of these types of love does God
express towards us, and expects us to express to Him
and others in kind? There's only one possible
answer: Agape, a love that is unconditional in all it
does. There are no requirements, pretexts,
limitations or other prior commitments necessary for
it to be expressed or to exist. How do I know this?
Take a look at these verses.

John 13:35 (KJV) - *"By this shall all men know that ye are my disciples, if ye have love one to another."*

John 21:16a (KJV) - *"He saith to him again the second time, Simon, son of Jonas, lovest thou me?"*

Matthew 22:37-40 (KJV) - *"Jesus said unto him, Thou shalt love the Lord thy God with all thy heart, and with all thy soul, and with all thy mind. This is the first and great commandment. And the second is like unto it, Thou shalt love thy neighbor as thyself. On these two commandments hang all the law and the prophets."*

In each of these verses, in the original Greek, the word used here for love is "Agape". God doesn't want us to just love Him and others if it suits our needs. He wants us to love everyone unconditionally. That means having faith and trust even where that may be impossible. But as has been said before, all things are possible through Christ. So if God commands us to show unconditional love towards one another (speaking of believers) and most especially to Him, doesn't it seem reasonable that something like that would indeed be possible? As such, even if we fall short, we should always try to love Him and others in the way that God loves us. Therefore if we have true love to both God and others, we must also have faith and trust in them. So in short, true love, as God has defined it, is always faithful, and always has faith.

POINTS FOR THOUGHT:

1. How much do I love God?
2. Does my faith and trust in Him show that?
3. Do I trust Him for my daily provision?
4. Do I love Him enough to trust everything He spoke of in His word, the Bible?
5. In what ways can I trust God more every day?
6. In what areas of my life, relating to God, do I lack trust?

LOVE ALWAYS HOPES, ALWAYS PERSEVERES

What is love without hope? Hope keeps us going every day of our lives. Hope is the single greatest energizer of perseverance. If we have hope, we will persevere. In many ways hope dovetails onto trust, because if we trust someone, we have faith that they'll come through for us. So in a way this can act as an extension or companion of trust. But what things in our life do we hope for? If we're saved and born again believers in Jesus Christ we have many things to hope for, such as Heaven, eternity with God the Father, Jesus Christ and the Holy Spirit, loved ones who have gone before us, and so much more. But don't we also have hope in Christ's current promises, and not just the future ones? Didn't Christ say he would never leave us or forsake us?

Deuteronomy 31:6 (NIV) - *"Be strong and courageous. Do not be afraid or terrified because of them, for the LORD your God goes with you; he will never leave you nor forsake you."*

Joshua 1:9 (KJV) - *"Have not I commanded thee? Be strong and of a good courage; be not afraid, neither be thou dismayed: for the LORD thy God [is] with thee whithersoever thou goest."*

Hebrews 13:5 (KJV) - *"Let your conversation be without covetousness; and be content with such things as ye have: for he hath said, I will never leave thee, nor forsake thee."*

Or what about the book of Revelation? Or Daniel? Or Ezekiel? They're all filled to the gills with prophesies and promises, such as this one:

Revelation 20:4 (KJV) - *"And I saw thrones, and they sat upon them, and judgment was given unto them: and I saw the souls of them that were beheaded for the witness of Jesus, and for the word of God, and which had not worshipped the beast, neither his image, neither had received his mark upon their foreheads, or in their hands; and they lived and reigned with Christ a thousand years."*

The bible is replete with promises like this, some fulfilled and some not. Of those that have been fulfilled, they clearly prove that God can be trusted in all things, including future events that have not yet occurred. In just my brief span of time on this planet I have already seen an incredible number of biblical prophesies and promises come to pass. In just the past seventy years alone we've seen the people of Israel return to their land (Isaiah 11:11-12), the nation of Israel being reborn (Isaiah 66:7-8 & Ezekiel 37:21-22), Jerusalem recaptured and reoccupied (Zechariah 8:4-8), the land returned from desolation to fruitfulness (Ezekiel 36:34-35), the Hebrew language revived from the dead and spoken again as a native language (Zephaniah 3:9), and Jerusalem becoming a city whose ownership is contested by the entire world (Zechariah 12:1-3).

And these are just a few of the prophesies that have come true in the past seventy years alone, with more either in progress or soon to be fulfilled at this very moment. And let's not forget the 350+ prophesies that Christ completely fulfilled in His first coming. But that's only the beginning. There's still a whole stack of them He's due to fill at His second coming. So if we know that He fulfilled every single prophecy pertaining to His first coming, how hard is it to believe that He will do the same when He comes the second time? Or what about all the things that He'll do after that time, or throughout eternity? God said it, He did it, and He will continue to do it. His track record is 100% so far and will remain so throughout eternity. If that doesn't give you hope, I don't know what will.

And through that hope we have perseverance, because who isn't motivated to hang on, to wait, to hold out hope and to trust in someone who has a perfect track record, who never fails, always perseveres, always remains faithful and never changes. If you love God, how can you not also hope and persevere, even through the greatest trials, with someone like that watching over you day and night? Remember, God never sleeps. So if you truly love someone you will always hope, always persevere. Just like the father of the prodigal son. Even though his youngest child was rebellious and had done great evil against him, he still persevered and held out hope until his child came home. We should not be expected to do any less.

POINTS FOR THOUGHT:

1. In what areas of my life do I lack hope and/or perseverance?
2. With whom do I lack either hope and/or perseverance?
3. If I've lost either, what can I do regain them?
4. Do I have hope in God and His promises? If I don't, what can I do to change this?

LOVE NEVER FAILS

So far we've covered all the other chief points spoken of by Paul in 1 Corinthians 13 that describes what true love is, and yet despite all this I believe the last point is, in my humble opinion, the best of them all. Why? It reminds us that, no matter what happens, true love never fails. So how do I know this to be true? God is the ultimate, unquestionable, absolute example of love, and being infinite and perfect He never has, no ever will fail us.

1 John 4:8 (NIV) - *"Whoever does not love does not know God, because God is love."*

Since God is love, if we know Him, we will in turn love Him. Maybe not as perfectly as He loves us, but we will love Him. But to love God perfectly we need to do so with all our heart, soul and mind, and we are to love others the same as we love ourselves. And if we love God as we should, the second requirement spoken of by Christ will be easy to do. But without love for God it is impossible to love others the way we should.

Matthew 22:37 (KJV) - *"Jesus said unto him, Thou shalt* *love the Lord thy God with all thy heart, and with all thy soul, and with all thy mind."*

In loving God as Jesus has commanded, we will in turn prove to others that love never fails, because if we keep all of these things in our lives and practice them daily, we will have the love that God commanded of us to have, and it will be so obvious that everyone will know it. But that kind of love is only possible if we're saved, because without Christ, love is not love, but rather a selfish action done with the intention of selfish gain. But if we are in Christ, we are a new creation, and all the old, selfish things are cast away, and for the first time in our lives we find ourselves able to express a true love that is not selfish, it is not self-serving, always seeks the betterment of others, and always loves.

Romans 8:38-39 (NIV) - *"For I am convinced that neither death nor life, neither angels nor demons, neither the present nor the future, nor any powers, neither height nor depth, nor anything else in all creation, will be able to separate us from the love of God that is in Christ Jesus our Lord."*

God's love is unconditional, therefore God's love will never fail. In turn, if we are saved, born again believers, God's love pours through us, and if we love God the way He has commanded that we should, our love will not fail either. But even if it should, we can always know with assurance that God's love will never fail, and that's what's most important.

POINTS FOR THOUGHT:

1. In what ways have I expressed my love for God to Him?
2. In what ways have I expressed my love of God to others?
3. In what ways have I expressed my love for others to them?
4. If I have not properly expressed my love to God and others, what must I do to change that?
5. What one thing can I do each day to show my love to God and others?
6. How can I live 24/7/365 expressing God's love to all?

LOVE IN THE 10 COMMANDMENTS

Exodus 20:3-17 (NIV) - *You shall have no other gods before[a] me. You shall not make for yourself an image in the form of anything in heaven above or on the earth beneath or in the waters below. You shall not bow down to them or worship them; for I, the LORD your God, am a jealous God, punishing the children for the sin of the parents to the third and fourth generation of those who hate me, but showing love to a thousand generations of those who love me and keep my commandments.*

You shall not misuse the name of the LORD your God, for the LORD will not hold anyone guiltless who misuses his name. Remember the Sabbath day by keeping it holy. 9 Six days you shall labor and do all your work, but the seventh day is a sabbath to the LORD your God. On it you shall not do any work, neither you, nor your son or daughter, nor your male or female servant, nor your animals, nor any foreigner residing in your towns.

For in six days the LORD made the heavens and the earth, the sea, and all that is in them, but he rested on the seventh day. Therefore the LORD blessed the Sabbath day and made it holy. Honor your father and your mother, so that you may live long in the land the LORD your God is giving you. You shall not murder. You shall not commit adultery. You shall not steal.

You shall not give false testimony against your neighbor. You shall not covet your neighbor's house. You shall not covet your neighbor's wife, or his male or female servant, his ox or donkey, or anything that belongs to your neighbor.

One of the most famous sections in the entire bible is the Ten Commandments. Almost everyone either knows them, or has heard of them. It's like John 3:16. Almost everyone knows that verse even if they're a hard core staunch atheist, or even the cruelest, most evil person in the entire world. But unlike John 3:16, when it comes to the Ten Commandments, they are among the most hated and despised verses in the world among the unsaved.

Why? Because they expose the three primary pillars of sin that are a part of everyone's life. Namely the lust of the flesh, the lust of the eyes, and the pride of life. They are, in the simplest terms, a guide to ten of the most important things one must do to be righteous before God. But did you know that when God gave Moses the Ten Commandments, they weren't meant to beat people over the head or "take all the fun out of life". Nor were they rules intended to make our lives miserable. The ten commandments are, much to the surprise of many, one of God's many love letters to mankind, with Jesus being the greatest of them all. Why is this? It's because the Ten Commandments are actually God's attempt to protect us from the ravages of sin.

In those ten laws are ten expressions of God's love to you. I'm pretty sure right now you're shaking your head thinking I'm crazy. But remember, one of the key elements of love is that it protects. In this case it's against the destructive ravages of sin. So by giving us these Ten Commandments, God is striving to keep us away from those sins that would otherwise destroy us, thus exercising an important element of love in the process. Namely that it protects what it loves. So God saying no doesn't mean He's being cruel and keeping you from having "fun". Instead He's doing it for your protection and to at the same time bless you. Just as an example, take a look at a couple of them and see what each does to keep you away from sin.

1. You shall have no other gods before Me.
This simple command calls people to put God first, thus executing the first part of the JOY principle.

5. Honor your father and your mother.
Love protects that which it loves. By honoring your father and your mother you are displaying love to them by doing them honor (ie, others before yourself,

part 2 of the JOY principle) and protecting them (i.e. shielding them from heartache and sadness) at the same time which again shows love.

6. You shall not murder.

Again, love protects that which it loves. With this God is protecting both you and others from the harmful effects of sin, namely death and the consequences it brings for the murderer.

And these are just a few of the examples of the love God expresses towards you, and through you to some degree, via the Ten Commandments. So they, like the law and other commandments of God, are not written to hurt you or be overbearing and cruel. They're done in love to protect you and others from the consequences and harmful effect of sin, and to remind you to keep God first in all things, others second and yourself last. And if you don't think that the Ten Commandments follows the JOY principle, take a look at how they're ordered. Commands 1-4 are about God and putting Him first. 5-10 are about others and yourself. Namely don't hurt others, and you won't be hurt yourself. So really, the Ten Commandments aren't really commandments in the sense of laws to be obeyed so much as they are a love letter reminding you to avoid sin and to love God and others above yourself, putting them first, and seeking true JOY in the process.

POINTS FOR THOUGHT:

1. Go through each of the Ten Commandments one by one and write down at least three ways in which God's love is expressed to you.
2. Find verses that show, reinforce, or illustrate how God demonstrates His love to you through the Ten Commandments.
3. Find ways in which you can apply both of these example in your daily life.
4. Thank God every day in prayer for each of these things you have written down.
5. Follow the Ten Commandments every day of your life to show your love to God.

THE CHURCH THAT LOST ITS FIRST LOVE

In the book of Revelation there is a narrative given starting in Chapter 2 and extending through Chapter 3 which talks about seven churches in Asia Minor, more specifically in the same land area as modern day Turkey and each of the things they've either gotten right, or are doing wrong. The first of the churches mentioned is Ephesus (Revelation 2:1-7) who the Lord Jesus at first praises because they have resisted the creep of false teachings into their midst, but then turns around and scolds only a verse later because they have lost their first love. Namely, they have become unloving and turned away from the love that they first had, a love they had received and learned from the Lord Jesus Himself.

Revelation 2:1-7 (KJV) - "*Unto the angel of the church of Ephesus write; These things saith he that holdeth the seven stars in his right hand, who walketh in the midst of the seven golden candlesticks; I know thy works, and thy labour, and thy patience, and how thou canst not bear them which are evil: and thou hast tried them which say they are apostles, and are not, and hast found them liars:*

And hast borne, and hast patience, and for my name's sake hast laboured, and hast not fainted. Nevertheless I have somewhat against thee, because thou hast left thy first love. Remember therefore from whence thou art fallen, and repent, and do the first works; or else I will come unto thee quickly, and will remove thy candlestick out of his place, except thou repent. But this thou hast, that thou hatest the deeds of the Nicolaitanes, which I also hate. He that hath an ear, let him hear what the Spirit saith unto the churches; To him that overcometh will I give to eat of the tree of life, which is in the midst of the paradise of God."

They were so zealous for God's law and commandments that in executing their duty to guard God's law, they lost their love for others. It's true that we are commanded to keep God's law. But we must also temper that with love. In other words we are to be obedient *in love*, and not "bible thumping" people as we so often do. The term "bible thumper" didn't come around just because we liked to thump our bibles on the table or pound our fingers on the verses within. No, we are quite often guilty of using our bibles to either figuratively or literally beat someone over the head. Instead of being loving to others, we would rather beat them with the law until they either are crushed, or fall into line.

That's not Christianity, nor is it loving. That's legalism, and it's something that Jesus spoke sternly against. He even repeatedly berated the Pharisees because of their rampant legalism. They upheld the law to the letter, but did so hatefully rather than lovingly. In fact, they even took their legalism a step further and began to create their own laws which superseded the commandments of God given in the bible, or in their case the Torah, as that's what it was called in their day. Laws should never have to be shoved down anyone's throat. If one truly loves the law giver, they will gladly and willingly obey the rules without question.

Another thing to consider is this. Those who truly love and trust God won't feel compelled to force others to obey. Believe it or not, forcing compliance on others is actually a sign of hatred to the other person. It's a proven fact that what you hate most in others is what you despise most in yourself. It's the idea of the beam and the speck that Jesus spoke about in Matthew 7:3-5.

Matthew 7:3-5 (NIV) - *"Why do you look at the speck of sawdust in your brother's eye and pay no attention to the plank in your own eye? How can you say to your brother, 'Let me take the speck out of your eye,' when all the time there is a plank in your own eye? You hypocrite, first take the plank out of your own eye, and then you will see clearly to remove the speck from your brother's eye."*

As one person put it, "The plank in your own eye causes you such pain and grief that you lash out in anger anytime you see someone else with that same sin, and you beat them over the head with your plank in hopes that doing so will dislodge it from your own eye and relieve your anguish." This isn't speaking of church discipline that seeks to restore the one caught in sin. This is rather the idea of assuaging one's own guilt and pain by beating another into submission. IE, rather than rising up to the level of another, you instead seek to drag them down to your own. That's what the Ephesians were doing. They weren't lovingly bringing people into obedience as God had directed. They were taking others who had a small twinkle of sin in their eye and crushed them.

If your child is disobedient, you don't beat them into a sniveling little pile of quivering flesh, do you? I should hope not. That's child abuse! So what do you do instead? You discipline them. This involves taking away privileges, freedoms, and so on in order to correct or eliminate a bad habit, punish a wrong action, and lovingly train up the child to understand that there are right ways to do things, and that wrong decisions have consequences. In doing so you create a well rounded, well behaved, intelligent human being who will go on to be a good adult. Love builds up, and good, commonsense discipline builds up the individual and strengthens them, and corrects their wrong actions despite a brief moment of uncomfortable chastisement.

That's the right way to do it. However, what the Ephesians, and ironically enough many Christians these days, did that drew Christ's rebuke was not proper discipline. They weren't trying to correct people who were living in sin. They were using the proverbial beams in their own eyes and beating others into submission. Hence why Christ said that they'd lost their first love. For a good, Godly description of proper handling of church discipline, study 1 Corinthians 5, and then follow it up with 2 Corinthians 2 to see the full process of church discipline and how it is best and properly handled in a kind and loving way. Remember, we are to love God and others in all things. If anything someone else is doing makes you angry, stop, look at it, and try to understand why it makes you angry.

What is it about what they're doing that causes you to become irate and, in some cases, legalistic with them? Look at it from the beam and speck perspective. Is what I'm angry at the other person for actually something I'm angry at myself for? I think if you take a deep look at the thing you're angry about and really study it closely, you'll find that you're more upset with yourself and your own sin than you are with theirs. When disciplining others we should do it in love. If we cannot, then we should withdraw and set our own lives right first, removing the sin from our own hearts, before we step forward and try to lovingly correct others, as Christ instructed us to do. Because we must always discipline in love, but never in anger.

POINTS FOR THOUGHT:

1. Am I in any way legalistic?
2. Is the reason for my legalism or anger to another because of the deep hatred I have for my own unresolved and unrepented sins?
3. Have I lost my first love? (ie, my love for Christ?)
4. If any of the above is true, what steps can I take to correct this?
5. How can I love God and others more every day?

LOVE IN THE BIBLE

Did you know that the word love appears in the King James version of the bible a total of 280 times. If you count in all the derivative versions (loves, loved, etc), it comes to a grand total of 442 times. In the NIV it appears 508 times by itself, or 697 times with its derivatives included. One of the greatest examples of love in the bible, aside from God's love for us through the death of His Son and the salvation He earned for us, is the love of a spouse. There are a number of great verses in the bible that speak of this, some from the Old Testament, and some from the New. Here's a few worth considering.

Genesis 29:20 (KJV) - *And Jacob served seven years for Rachel; and they seemed unto him [but] a few days, for the love he had to her.*

Ephesians 5:25 (KJV) - *Husbands, love your wives, even as Christ also loved the church, and gave himself for it;*

The book of Ruth also shows many great examples of love to a mother in law, to God, and to a future husband or wife. But of all the books in the bible, Song of Solomon is probably the single best one in regards to the marital relationship. It gets seriously mushy, and a bit explicit in places, but if you're ever in need of something to help you supercharge your married life, I recommend reading that book all the way through from cover to cover. Psalms is also book full of love passages. For example the following is a great statement of love for God.

Psalm 18:1 (KJV) - *I will love these, O Lord, my strength.*

It's written by David, and tells of his absolute love and devotion to God, and the realization that he can't live without God being part of every corner of his life, including his very strength. But this is only one facet in a great big gem of love found in this book, and every other book in the bible. Take for example the words of Jesus from Luke.

Luke 6:35 (NIV) - *But love your enemies, do good to them, and lend to them without expecting to get anything back. Then your reward will be great, and you will be sons of the Most High, because he is kind to the ungrateful and wicked.*

In a sense it's a nutshell version of Matthew 22:37-40. Even so, this isn't anywhere near all of it.

I've only begun to touch on the topic of love as it's displayed and discussed in the bible. Love is everywhere, on every chapter, on every page, and if you aren't reading your bible regularly you're missing out on one of the best expressions of God's love ever written. God even very strongly encourages us to read our bible, as it's His word to us and will help strengthen and reinforce our lives, drawing us closer to Him every day. But even beyond that and above all else, the bible is God's love letter to us. So why not read it every day, even several times a day, because the love of God is without limit or measure, poured out and overflowing. He wants to share His love for you every minute of every day, and desires you, His child, to love Him in return.

POINTS FOR THOUGHT:

1. Find every passage or verse you can about love in the bible.
2. How do each of these apply to your life?
3. Thank God for His infinite love to you every day in your prayers.
4. Tell God regularly how much you love Him.
5. Demonstrate to God and others how much you love Him through your daily actions and service to Him and to others.

LOVE THE HELL OUT OF THE LOST

A while back one of my friends at church mentioned something to me about the way we should witness to people. They said, "We should love the Hell out of them." The idea of their words was not to express a profanity laced triad, but rather that we should love people so much that we would do all we possibly could to win them to Christ and save them from an eternity in Hell. Or as C. H. Spurgeon once said, "*Oh, my brothers and sisters in Christ, if sinners will be damned, at least let them leap to hell over our bodies; and if they will perish, let them perish with our arms about their knees, imploring them to stay, and not madly to destroy themselves. If hell must be filled, at least let it be filled in the teeth of our exertions, and let not one go there unwarned and unprayed for.*"

If we truly loved others, we'd be down on our knees every day and every night praying for and witnessing to the lost, imploring them to come to Christ, and doing everything we possibly could to keep them out of Hell. But if we won't, or refuse to, perhaps it's because we don't really understand the true horrors of Hell. If we did, we wouldn't wish for even our worst enemies to go there.

2 Thessalonians 1:9 (KJV) - *"They will be punished with everlasting destruction and shut out from the presence of the Lord and from the majesty of his power."*

Matthew 13:50 (KJV) - *"and throw them into the fiery furnace, where there will be weeping and gnashing of teeth."*

Luke 16:24 (KJV) - *"And he called out, 'Father Abraham, have mercy on me, and send Lazarus to dip the end of his finger in water and cool my tongue, for I am in anguish in this flame.'"*

Revelation 14:11 (KJV) - *"And the smoke of their torment goes up forever and ever, and they have no rest, day or night, these worshipers of the beast and its image, and whoever receives the mark of its name."*

While these verses don't draw a good, clear picture of how terrible Hell is, even what little is there should be enough to drive you to your knees and thank Christ for dying to save you, and for His gift of salvation that saved you from Hell. If you haven't accepted Christ as your savior, you should, because Hell, despite what people may say, is a place that nobody should want to go to, or should ever have to. But as we all have free will, it's our choice if we wish to accept Christ's payment for our sins through His death, burial and resurrection, or reject it in our pride and be cast forever into a fire and a torment beyond imagination that will never end.

And I know that we live in a very visually oriented society these days, and I know these two resources are extra-biblical (ie, outside the cannon of scripture), however I think they're worth your time to look into. The first comes from Bill Wiese. He's produced a complete series surrounding a core topic titled "23 Minutes In Hell". Bill is a very Godly man and a strong Christian, but from what I've gathered by his presentations, God took him to Hell for a time and showed him around, and even allowed him to experience the horrors of that place so that he could come back and warn others that Hell is not only real, but somewhere you absolutely do not want to go to. Ever. It's not even a place you'd want to send your worst, most hated enemy. Yes, it's that bad. At the time I'm writing this he's posted a copy of the core DVD around which the entire series pivots via his Youtube channel. A simple search for the sermon title will bring it up.

The video itself, about an hour long, is a presentation done in Johannesburg, South Africa in front of a live studio audience detailing Hell as he experienced it. There's also another person, a lady named Mary K. Baxter, who had a similar experience, and her message is haunting. If you listen to both of them and it doesn't change your life, and give you a true understanding of how horrible Hell is, then you need to do a heart check. But once you've watched both, then you need to ask yourself this question. What will you do with this information? Would you want anyone you know to go to Hell because of your apathy, your laziness, inaction, or worse yet, your lack of love? If you love others, and especially God, you will do all you can to love them into Heaven, to witness to them and as Spurgeon said, if they are to go to Hell, let them be made to leap over our bodies, because Christ loves all of us and wants none of us to go to Hell. Period.

1 Timothy 2:4 (KJV) - *"Who will have all men to be saved, and to come unto the knowledge of the truth."*

2 Peter 3:9 (KJV) - *"The Lord is not slack concerning his promise, as some men count slackness; but is longsuffering to us-ward, not willing that any should perish, but that all should come to repentance."*

POINTS FOR THOUGHT:

1. Do you love the people around you enough that you would do all within your power to keep them from falling into Hell unsaved and lost forever?
2. If not, what can you do to change that?

ARE YOU HIS CHILD?

Are you a born again child of God? Have you accepted Jesus as your Lord and Savior? If not, then let me ask you a question. Has this book opened your eyes to the current state of your life and revealed to you that you are not only a sinner (we all are), but in need of the free salvation that Jesus offers? Or perhaps you felt or thought that you were saved, but through reading this book you've discovered that you're anything but redeemed? If your life doesn't reflect the loving nature of God, and especially of Christ, you may not be saved. We may not be able to love God as perfectly as He loves us, but if we are His children, His saved and redeemed people, His ecclesia or "called out ones", our lives should reflect it. If you know you're not saved, or question if you are, please read through the following questions and then decide for yourself.

1. **Romans 3:23 (KJV)**: *for all have sinned and fallen short of the glory of God.*

All have sinned. Every single one of us. We're born as sinners, and we spend our entire lives in sin. No amount of self-righteousness or good works can change that. If anything, it makes it worse. So ask yourself this. Have you ever lied? I'm not talking about big fat lies. I'm talking about any kind of lie, even the teeny tiniest white lie. A lie is a sin, no matter what 'size' we place on it. What about stealing? We've all stolen at one time or another. Have we lusted after someone else who wasn't our spouse? If you're human, yes you have, no matter who you are.

So right there are three big sins that'll keep you out of Heaven and separate you from God. It only requires you committing one sin to send you to Hell. Just one. Yet we do tens, hundreds, and possibly even thousands of sins per day. If we sin that often, what hope do we have of being righteous and perfect enough to get into Heaven. We don't.

James 2:10: *For whosoever shall keep the whole law, and yet offend in one [point], he is guilty of all.*

All sins carry the same weight with God. So by committing even one teeny tiny, itty bitty sin, you're officially brought down to the same spiritual level as some of history's most evil men, such as the likes of Adolf Hitler and Stalin. To think yourself to be spiritually better than anyone else is wrong, because every sinner is equal in God's eyes. Every one of us has sinned, and therefore we are all guilty and deserving of judgment, no matter who we are.

2. **Romans 6:23**: *For the wages of sin is death, but the gift of God is eternal life through Christ Jesus our Lord.*

The Bible states it clearly. We sin, we die. Period. It doesn't matter how great or small we are, who we might be, how much money we may have, or anything. There's no dividing line in God's word, no social classes or nationalities. If we sin, we earn the penalty of death, both spiritually and physically, which means eternity in Hell. It's no different than if we commit a crime. If you were to rob a store, what would happen to you? Well, you'd go to jail. So if we expect a criminal to be punished for what they've done, how can we not expect God to do the same when we sin?

We can't. That means since we've sinned, we're guilty and deserving of punishment. And, that punishment is death. Eternal death. Burning in Hell forever. However, take note of the latter part of the verse where it says *"but the gift of God is eternal life through Christ Jesus our Lord."* Doesn't that give you at least a little bit of hope? Yes, we've sinned and deserve to die as punishment for what we've done, and yet God gave us a way out; a "get out of jail free" card if you will, through the death of His Son, Jesus

Christ, on the cross. But there's more. Read on.

3. **Romans 5:8**: *But God demonstrates his own love for us in this: That while we were yet sinners, Christ died for us.*

Isn't that fabulous news!? God loves us so much that, even though we've sinned, He allowed His only Son to be sacrificed so that we might be saved! If any of you who are reading this have kids, I'm certain you know how hard it is to release them into today's scary world. You just want to hold them tight, watch over them, and protect them from all harm and danger.

But if you had the chance to save someone, possibly even millions or billions of people, would you be willing to sacrifice the life of your own child to do it? I believe the answer of almost every parent would be no. And yet God did. What should that say to us about how much He loves us? What God gave you is an incredible expression of love. Unconditional love. Love without boundaries, limits or stipulations. Agape love as the Greeks call it.

God loved you so much that He provided you with a way to be saved. Would you turn away from something so incredibly wonderful? Would you say no to what God has done for you? God loves you so much that He made a way for your sins to be forgiven, and for you to be reconciled to Him. And He did it in a way that proved without a doubt His love for you.

4. **Romans 10:9-10**: *That if you confess with your mouth, "Jesus is Lord," and believe in your heart that God raised Him from the dead, you will be saved. For it is with your heart that you believe and are justified, and it is with your mouth that you confess and are saved.*

As the verse says, salvation is simple. Almost too simple as many people believe. In fact it's so simple that many reject it, instead turning to their works based ideology that says "I have to earn my way to heaven" and try to apply it to salvation through Jesus. They say, "It can't be that simple!" And yet it is. All it takes is to accept the gift that Jesus earned for you through His death and resurrection, putting your complete and total trust in Him, a full and total repentance (turning away) from *ALL* your sins (even the little "pet" or "innocent" ones), and a simple belief that God raised Jesus from the dead to save you from your sins, you will be saved. There is no guessing, and there is no doubt. If you truly believe, you truly repent of your sins, you accept what Jesus has done for you on the cross, and you put your full and complete trust in Him, you ***will be saved***.

Now if you can read these words with joy, and know without a doubt that you're already saved, I praise God for you! But if you can't, then know that God is calling out to you, beckoning for you to come to Him. As such, will you accept His gift, and His calling of you to repentance? Or will you reject it, choosing to remain in your sins, covered by your nicely tailored suits, or your beautiful dresses? Salvation doesn't come by inheritance, nor does it come by association. It doesn't matter what church you attend, what denomination you belong to, or whether your parents believed. God has no grandchildren. Every person must make the decision to accept Christ on their own.

God loves you, but your sin separates you from Him. God is holy and without fault, and He cannot look upon sin. But He still loves you, regardless of what you've done. He created you, and you are His child, and He wants to start a relationship with you today. Will you surrender your pride and sin, and accept His gift of salvation, and eternal life? If your answer is yes, then read on.

The most important thing you must understand about salvation is that it's a gift, and just like any gift, it must be accepted before it can become yours. So how do you accept this gift? Simple. In your own words, pray now and admit to Jesus that you are a sinner, that you believe that He died and rose again for your sins, that you accept His gift of eternal life and that you put your entire trust in Him. If you've already done that at some time in the past, then this exploration of salvation has merely been a confirmation of your belief. But if you were not a believer before, and have just prayed and believed today, then praise God, and welcome to the family!

The next thing to do now is to step out in faith, prepare yourself, and then move forward to serve God as He has commanded each of us to do. If you find yourself as a new believer, it's a good idea to find another Christian, or perhaps a good local church, and using the Bible as your guide, grow in your new found faith, and prepare yourself for the work that God has waiting for you. But if you're already a believer, then this book will merely be a guidepost to the ways you should live your life, and most especially, how you must love God with all your heart, soul, and mind, and others as yourself, and well as the many wonderful ways in which you can do that.

GO AND LOVE AS GOD COMMANDED

Whether you're already a believer, or just became one, God commands us to love one another, be they great or small, young or old, enemy or friend, and to love Him most of all. So go out into the world and spread the love of God by showing love to others. To those you've hated, been jealous or envious of, whom you've hurt, dishonored, or done anything unloving or unkind, seek their forgiveness, and then love them as Christ loved us.

OTHER WRITINGS BY AUTHOR STEVEN LAKE

MANNA
Trusting in the Provisions of God

THE GREAT COMMISSION
Answering God's Call To Missions

JENNA'S JOURNEY
A Journey To A New Beginning